Baby Animals in the Wild!

Monkey Infants in the Wild

by Marie Brandle

Bullfrog Books

Ideas for Parents and Teachers

Bullfrog Books let children practice reading informational text at the earliest reading levels. Repetition, familiar words, and photo labels support early readers.

Before Reading

- Discuss the cover photo. What does it tell them?

- Look at the picture glossary together. Read and discuss the words.

Read the Book

- "Walk" through the book and look at the photos. Let the child ask questions. Point out the photo labels.

- Read the book to the child, or have him or her read independently.

After Reading

- Prompt the child to think more. Ask: Monkey infants walk and run. How else do they get around?

Bullfrog Books are published by Jump!
5357 Penn Avenue South
Minneapolis, MN 55419
www.jumplibrary.com

Library of Congress Cataloging-in-Publication Data

Names: Brandle, Marie, 1989– author.
Title: Monkey infants in the wild / by Marie Brandle.
Description: Minneapolis, MN: Jump!, Inc., [2023]
Series: Baby animals in the wild! | Includes index.
Audience: Ages 5–8
Identifiers: LCCN 2022010062 (print)
LCCN 2022010063 (ebook)
ISBN 9798885240772 (hardcover)
ISBN 9798885240789 (paperback)
ISBN 9798885240796 (ebook)
Subjects: LCSH: Monkeys—Infancy—Juvenile literature.
Classification: LCC QL737.P925 B73 2023 (print)
LCC QL737.P925 (ebook)
DDC 599.813/92—dc23/eng/20220315
LC record available at https://lccn.loc.gov/2022010062
LC ebook record available at https://lccn.loc.gov/2022010063

Editor: Eliza Leahy
Designer: Molly Ballanger

Photo Credits: EcoPrint/Shutterstock, cover; marcelauret/iStock, 1; Anders Riishede/Shutterstock, 3; Sam Dcruz/Shutterstock, 4, 23tr; elisevonwinkle/Shutterstock, 5, 23br; aroundtheworld.photography/Alamy, 6–7, 23bl; James Hager/Robert Harding Picture Library/SuperStock, 8; Nick Fox/Shutterstock, 9; Barbara von Hoffmann/Alamy, 10–11; dja Photography/Shutterstock, 12–13; Morales/age fotostock/SuperStock, 14–15; AfricaWildlife/Shutterstock, 16; Michel Bureau/Biosphoto/SuperStock, 17, 23tl; Tony Campbell/Shutterstock, 18–19; imageBROKER.com/Shutterstock, 20–21; DUFORETS BERANGERE/Shutterstock, 22; Manon van Althuis/Shutterstock, 24.

Printed in the United States of America at Corporate Graphics in North Mankato, Minnesota.

Table of Contents

Monkeying Around

A baboon infant is born.
It is a kind of monkey.

It lives with Mom in a troop.
The troop has many infants!

troop

The baboons live on the savanna.

They look for food.

savanna

The infant can walk.

But it moves faster on Mom's back.

It holds on.

It uses its hands and feet.

They find bugs.
They eat them!

Mom cleans the infant.
She picks bugs off its fur.

fur

The infant grows.
It runs.
It plays.

It jumps.

It climbs.

Its tail helps it balance.

tail

It swings from branches!
It uses its long arms.

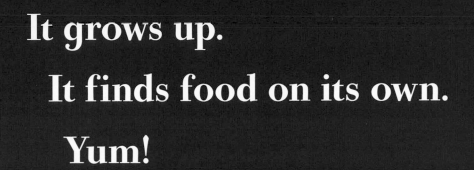

It grows up.

It finds food on its own.

Yum!

Parts of a Monkey Infant

What are the parts of a monkey infant? Take a look!

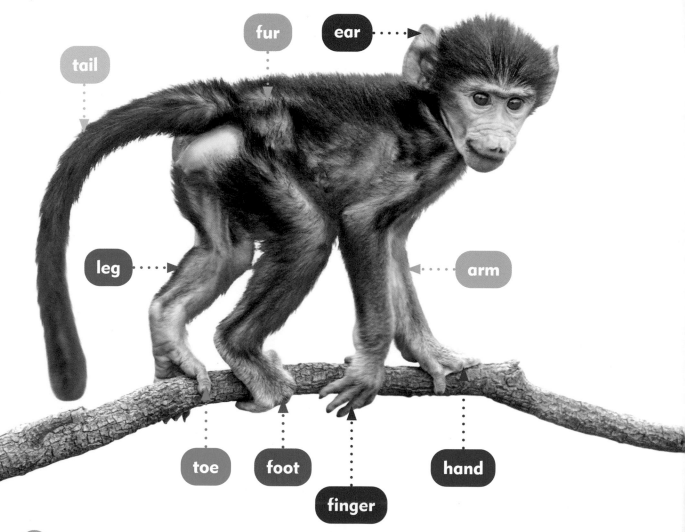

fur

ear

tail

leg

arm

toe

foot

finger

hand

Picture Glossary

balance
To stay steady and upright.

infant
A young monkey.

savanna
A flat, grassy plain with few or no trees.

troop
A group of monkeys.

Index

To Learn More

Finding more information is as easy as 1, 2, 3.

❶ Go to www.factsurfer.com

❷ Enter "monkeyinfants" into the search box.

❸ Choose your book to see a list of websites.